Will you come with me?

Sharilyn Schultz

Illustrations by

Telma Pereira

Balboa Press books may be ordered through booksellers or by contacting:

Balboa Press
A Division of Hay House
1663 Liberty Drive
Bloomington, IN 47403
www.balboapress.com
844-682-1282

Because of the dynamic nature of the Internet, any web addresses or links contained in this book may have changed since publication and may no longer be valid. The views expressed in this work are solely those of the author and do not necessarily reflect the views of the publisher, and the publisher hereby disclaims any responsibility for them.

Any people depicted in stock imagery provided by Getty Images are models, and such images are being used for illustrative purposes only.
Certain stock imagery © Getty Images.

ISBN: 979-8-7652-5492-9 (sc)
ISBN: 979-8-7652-5485-1 (e)

Library of Congress Control Number: 2024917305

Print information available on the last page.

Balboa Press rev. date: 04/03/2025

Will you come with me?

I need something.

2

3

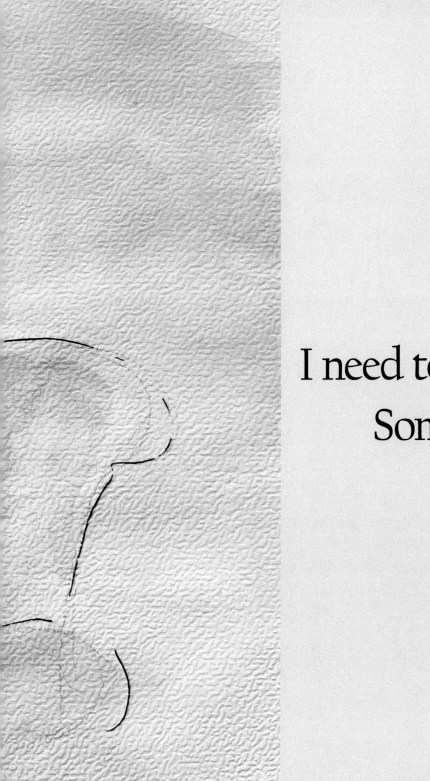

I need to go somewhere.
Someplace safe.

Will you come
with me?

I don't want to go
all by myself.
I feel scared.

Will you come
with me?

I don't really know
where I want to go......

I just want to
feel safe.
And happy.
And loved.

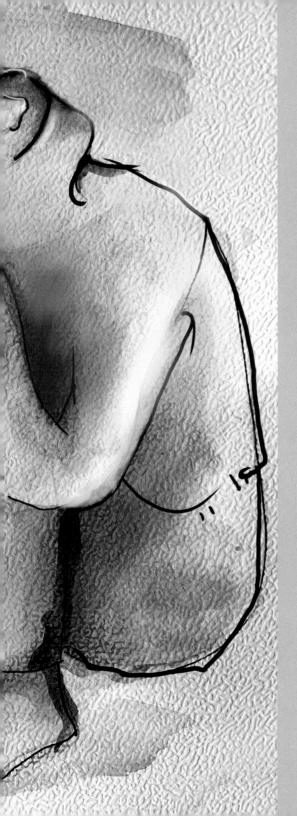

I want to know
you care.
I want to know
you love me
no matter what.

16

I feel loved
when you hold me close
and tell me
you're here for me.

I feel loved when
you just listen
to me talk.
It doesn't matter
what I'm
talking about.
Just listen!

I feel safe when you respect my feelings. Even if you don't understand them. And especially when you do.

Just listen.

25

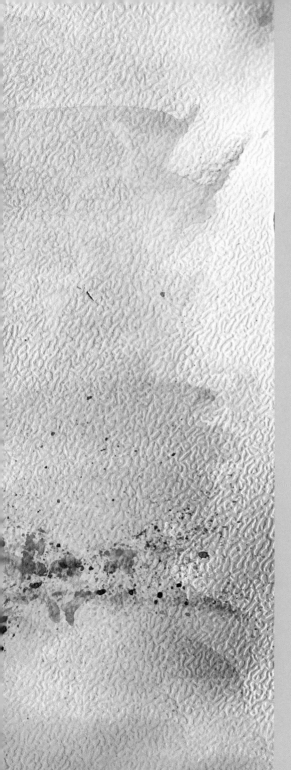

Will you come with me
to my safe place?

Will you be
there with me?
Just there,
listening,
holding me.
Holding love in
that space.

Will you do that
for me?

I really need a
safe place.
I really need to know
that I'm loved
unconditionally.

I need to just *be.*

34

Will you come
with me?

Because
my safe place

is *You.*

Printed in the United States
by Baker & Taylor Publisher Services